T0209820

EVERYDAY
JOY AND
TACOS

A 28-DAY GUIDE TO CREATE A JOYFUL LIFE

AMY KLENE

BALBOA
PRESS

A DIVISION OF HAY HOUSE

Balboa Press books may be ordered through booksellers or by contacting:

Balboa Press
A Division of Hay House
1663 Liberty Drive
Bloomington, IN 47403
www.balboapress.com
1 (877) 407-4847

Print information available on the last page.

ISBN: 978-1-9822-1785-3 (sc)
ISBN: 978-1-9822-1787-7 (hc)
ISBN: 978-1-9822-1786-0 (e)

Library of Congress Control Number: 2018914590

Balboa Press rev. date: 12/11/2018

Dedicated to my tribe.
Without you, I could not have found my joy.

CONTENTS

CHAPTER 1
INTRODUCTION

Joy. The word captured my attention early in my life as it is literally my middle name. As a child, I was teased around Christmas time with taunts of bringing (or not bringing) joy to the world. In Junior High Algebra class, I had a substitute teacher (you know the cringeworthy ones who read first, middle, and last names for attendance) disclose my joyful middle name, and a new student who moved to Colorado from Michigan exclaimed, "AMY JOY? Like the Doughnut place in Michigan?" My mom was from Michigan but Amy Joy Doughnuts never came up in our conversations about my name selection. Later that day, I asked my mom if she named me after Amy Joy Doughnuts and she paused and insinuated she may have done it *indirectly*. I have to believe it could have been worse; doughnuts are pretty delicious.

Because of this, the topic of joy has been on my mind as long as I can remember. I have long tried to understand the difference between happiness and joy and have come across some great perspectives on the differences some asserting that joy is a moment in time and that happiness is a state of well-being. Some schools of thought declare happiness and joy are the same thing. Some say you can be joyful without being happy and that happiness can exist without joy. My position is a little different and I believe that joy not only lives in happiness, but joy is the key, the life preserver, to get out of sadness. I believe that with the right mindset and perspective, joy exists in our brightest and darkest times; joy is the key to unlocking our divine nature and understanding our divine love.

As I continued to contemplate joy over my many years, different situations brought about or took away joy and I wondered how that could happen. Different people brought out joy within me and others very clearly, brought out the less joyful aspects of myself. I realized I had to choose joy and create joy and surround myself with joy focused people to grow and live a happiness focused life. The minute I stopped choosing joy was the moment my life would go off road.

The Miriam Webster definition of joy is the emotion evoked by well-being, success, or good fortune or by the prospect of possessing what one desires : delight; the expression or exhibition of such emotion: gaiety a state of happiness or felicity : bliss. I believe joy is more than just an emotion, I believe it is in our DNA like little keys to unlock the deeper wisdoms of our true self, deeper wisdoms and mysteries. I believe joy once fully realized is the tool to get each of us to the next level of our human potential. Without choosing and creating joy in our lives, we stagnate or move away from our growth and purpose.

To date, my findings on joy are included in what you hold in your hand and I hope my activities around joy bring you great joy, and help you determine your creative path to a joyful life.

What response does the word "joy" elicit in you? Does the word joy feel light, childish or fluffy to you, or does it feel like joy is for other people, or that you don't deserve it? I ask this to make sure we are clear as you begin this journey and for you to understand exactly where your starting point is. You may already be fully immersed in a life filled with joy and healthy habits to make choices aligned with your higher self and this book will just be a new way to create habits to deeply realize and continue to create joy. Or, this book will help you remove beliefs and blocks about allowing joy to flow into your life effortless and easily as we are all meant to experience. Really pause and think about your position on joy right now or if you even have one yet. Who or what brings you great joy, and who or what can make your joy disappear?

In June of 2018, we took a little vacation to Boston. I was sitting on a train with my daughter and husband heading to the North End of Boston for life changing Italian food and I saw a woman with a t-shirt on that said "Tacos make everything better." I looked around the train at the faces of each train compadre and couldn't help but be overwhelmed by the diversity from ethnicity to age to socioeconomic position, and her shirt was something that applied to all of us – tacos, or something that brings us joy and happiness, DOES make everything better. The questions that came to me on the train ride were, "Do we each really know what the thing is that makes everything better for us? If it isn't tacos, what is it that does make everything better? And why don't we all eat more tacos – or do the things that bring us joy and happiness more consistently? What if there was a guide to joy that fit in our day effortlessly that brought about that taco-eating-feeling. Would our lives feel a little more connected, happy, and fulfilled?" That small subtle interaction turned into the book you hold in your hands today. I want to thank the taco shirt wearing woman and hope she is blessed with bottomless tacos all the days of her life.

JOY IN GRIEF

2001 was a game changing year for myself and my family. I had been a technical writer for my company for 5 years and was promoted to

3

Technical Publications manager that year. My husband was starting his Master's degree program, we had 2 beautiful healthy amazing boys (Ian and Logan) who were 4 and 2 and we moved into the neighborhood my husband and I wanted to live in as children. Side note: we lived and still live in the same hometown where we both grew up in Colorado. My husband was teaching History and coaching football and life was humming along with lots to be grateful for. we were living our dreams as exhausting as they were on some days. In July, we found out our little tribe was expanding which we were not expecting, but were so excited to add another personality to our life. We headed down the path we had been on 2 times before and started to make room for the baby in our new nest and in our hearts.

The fall of that same year, the tragedy of 9/11 happened, one of my closest friends lost her mom, and on October 22nd, I went into early labor. When we arrived at the hospital, they were certain the baby wouldn't make it out of the operating room alive and we were told to prepare for the worst outcome. Jason Andrew was born with insurmountable health issues but did make it out of the operating room alive and we were able to spend 4 amazing days with him at Children's Hospital in Denver. I will tell you that in the middle of grief there are moments where you are present in a way you aren't in your daily life. You are faced with a decision to choose light or dark, love or despair, joy or sadness, and you see your strength in a new light. I remember looking at Jason and realizing I was faced with a choice of grieving while he was here, or grieving after he was gone so I dug deep and was present with him and truly consciously enjoyed every minute. I made a deliberate choice to find those life preservers of joy while just sitting with him, reading to him, telling him about his brother's crazy adventures - I made a conscious decision and chose joy.

We had so many visitors that week that the hospital had to create a waiting list for people to come back a few at a time to be with us in the NICU. Friends and family left notes and the boys drew Jason pictures we put up all around his crib. In those 4 days, we created so much love around that beautiful baby that when it was time for us to remove life support, I knew we had done everything we could to give him a lifetime of love in his brief time here with us.

I share this story not to be sad. I share this story to demonstrate how the big things in life that are obvious successes build a foundation for when we are impacted by grief, loss, tragedy, and despair. The foundation you build with the people in your life, the tribe we get to create and are born into, come along with us in the joy and are with us in the sadness. That connection to each other actually helps to heal our emotional, mental, and spiritual pain. Think about a time when you were grieving or sad and your best friend just came over to be with you. The presence of your person made all the difference without saying a word or doing something extravagant. Showing up for each other in grief and sadness is joy in action – a life preserver.

As you look for the joy life preservers in grief, you will notice the people in your life that love you are constantly rooting for you to find the happiness and only temporarily visit the sadness; not live there. We want that for the people we love too when they are hurting. We want them to acknowledge the grief, but also look to us for healing and love.

How many times do we lose sight of how precious every day really is? My experience with Jason was my wake up call to stay awake and be present with everyone in my life. It was a gift Jason gave me and continues to give me whenever I am not choosing joy.

It goes without saying that the experience of Jason broke not only myself wide open, it impacted the entire tribe of people that cared for myself, my husband and my boys. We took it day by day for a very long time and continued to heal from the impact of losing our son. In February 2004, 2 and a half years after Jason's birthday, our beautiful daughter Megan Joy was born happy and healthy and was a perfect grand finale for us. Her addition to our lives has been such a joy and I couldn't help but pass on the middle name.

I challenge you to think about grief in your life and look for the moments that kept you going, the moments where love surfaced out of nowhere or someone reached out unexpectedly at just the right time. All of those moments are filled with powerful love, and have the capacity to bring a joyful perspective in time. Joy lives in both happiness and sadness equally. One is just much easier to access, but never doubt it is there.

HOW TO USE THE BOOK

This book is intended to be simple, straight forward, and effortless. The 28 days map to the 7 chakras in your being. Those 7 chakras then correspond to the 7 days of the week encouraging you to focus your attention on one chakra a day with 7 different fun activities. The time investment each day is minimal, maybe 10 – 15 minutes, and the financial investment is also minimal; maybe the cost of a cup of coffee here and there but the intention is to have the activities fit easily into your life.

I am a firm believer that structure is actually the mother of creativity. Without structure first, creative energy cannot be concentrated and focused. For example, what would it be like to drive if there were no roads, no agreement that green lights mean go, and that red did not indicate you need to stop – not that everyone agrees on that 100% anyway. There would be total chaos and instead of getting where you need to go quickly and efficiently, you would be angry, frustrated or worse consistently injured because everyone would be crashing into each other. We would not feel safe and would not be able to go where we needed to go with ease. The book is a 28 day practice to create a road system for joy in your life that you get to design and build. Within each day are 7 very simple activities to get your imagination going.

Research shows that it takes 21 – 66 days to create a habit that sticks, so the book includes a month's worth of ideas to try on and make your own. The more consistent you are with making time for the joyful mindfulness activities, the more consistent your results will be. You can always pick it up at any time. I have learned as a parent, partner, and friend that being consistent makes all the difference in healthy relationships. Why not be consistent with the most important relationship you will ever have – the relationship with yourself.

The 7 activities or ideas for each day are designed to be like a light switch for you each morning as you wake up and begin your new adventure each day. Every day is unique and even when we feel we are in a rut and every day is the same, that is actually our irrational brain taking over. Every sunrise is new, the weather is always different, your body is regenerating, your thoughts are always new and you have the opportunity each day to exercise your free will to either continue with the same, or try something new even if it is reading a new book, blog, coffee shop; you can create a new experience at any time.

Choosing to create new experiences creates joy and excitement in your being and wakes your mind up and connects your conscious mind to your super conscious mind where the good stuff happens. Your creativity, connection to the divine, your higher self all live in the super conscious. Tapping into that part of your mind, and bringing that energy to your conscious self creates joy, happiness, and a sense of center and balance. The 28 days (1 months' worth of activities), is meant to help you connect and stay connected to a steady stream of joy. When you feel happy and joyful, you will inspire others to do the same and in spreading that joy you will do your part in bringing love to the planet and we all desperately need you to bring your joy and shine that beautiful light.

CHAKRAS

We are all made up of energy and are constantly in motion. Even when we are sleeping, our minds are still going, our organs are all working – we are a 24 x 7 operation if we are conscious or not. It is seriously amazing when you stop and think about it.

The translation of the word chakra means "wheel" and is a metaphor for the sun. The oldest written tradition of the chakra energy system dates back to India in 1,500 to 500 BC. It represents the eternal wheel of time which represents celestial order and balance. For a visualization, imagine colored polka dots down the center of your body when you think of your chakras. The energy goes out in front of you and also behind you. When you chakras are balanced, you are able to heal, thrive, and grow. When your energy is out of balance, illness, disease, sadness, anxiety can set in. Keeping our energy balanced should be a priority for all of us.

This very high level explanation is the tip of the iceberg of information on chakras and there are many resources and cultural references on chakras, but for our purpose and intention to create a joy practice, this information I am including is a good starting point. The subsequent chapters in the book will have different information and practices around working with the chakras.

Included is a high level overview of each chakra, the color associated with the energy, where they are in your body, and high level meaning:

- **Root Chakra** – lower abdomen - Red – Connection to earth – Sense of Survival
- **Sacral Chakra** – mid abdomen - Orange - Creativity
- **Solar Plexus Chakra** – mid body/ lungs - Yellow – Self Esteem and Self Confidence
- **Heart Chakra** – heart - Green, Pink, White - Love of self, love of others, love of all
- **Throat Chakra** – neck - sky blue – Speak your personal truth
- **3rd Eye Chakra,** Indigo – middle of the forehead - Spiritual sight – Focus on intuition
- **Crown Chakra** – top of head - White – Connection to Spirit

THE 7 DAILY ACTIVITIES

FORECAST AND WEATHER CHECK

We are constantly processing emotions either in a healthy way or in a not so healthy way. We can look at emotions like a weather report each day and detach a bit from feeling overwhelmed by strong emotions. For example, if we are able to wake up in the morning, and check in with ourselves in an open and honest way, we will yield better results. If we know we are going to have to have a hard conversation with someone, we can prepare differently if we plan for it and the outcome has potential to be more positive if we bring a healthy perspective to the conversation. As an example, you can in the morning say to yourself "I can do this!", you can declare an intention, "My intention is to deliver this message with kindness and compassion", and your mantra can be "I speak my truth." Your mind and energy is aligned to be positive, loving and kind. The flip side creates a storm of self-doubt and self-deprecation that makes the difficult conversation even more difficult and you may completely talk yourself out of having the conversation all together perpetuating a negative pattern in your life. How you show up for yourself will always be your choice. No one can make that choice or take that choice from you.

If you are in the middle of your day and become triggered, let people know you feel a little "stormy" and take time to get centered opposed to taking your storm out on people. You will usually regret demonstrating your explosive side and later that behavior negatively impacts relationships if people have the courage to tell you or not. We have all done this. Know you don't have to keep processing the emotion of anger by pushing it down and watching it erupt later. You are not your emotions, but your emotions are signals of what you need to heal, process, or let go. It is much easier to enjoy a sunny day opposed to a rainy one, but we need them both to grow. Acting like the sun is always out is inauthentic to human nature, so honor your emotions, let them pass, and keep the storm as contained as possible. Always pack an umbrella.

MANTRA

A mantra is a daily anthem to help the mind stay focused on something positive. Think of your daily mantra as your motto for the day. For example, if it is Tuesday and you are focusing your mindfulness practice on your throat chakra and gratitude, your mantra for the day of "I speak my truth" will help you stay focused on speaking up for yourself, and giving gratitude to others. You can say it silently or out loud, whichever is most helpful. Mantras help create an anchor. You can always change the mantras to best fit you and what is happening in your day.

This past summer I had a great opportunity to do yoga with my neighbors in an incredible location – Red Rocks Amphitheater in Morrison, Colorado. There were hundreds of people with bright colored yoga mats dotting the amphitheater rows and in center stage was the yoga instructor. We began stretching and she started to share a story of when she was first practicing yoga in the 1990's. She said she wasn't dressed in the right attire, didn't know the poses and felt like a fish out of water. She said that she kept telling herself during class that she didn't belong, that she wasn't good enough, and that she should never come back. However, by the end of the class she had such a sense of peace and well-being that she realized she did indeed belong and that it was her habit of negative self-talk and her inner critic that was trying to stop her from enjoying the experience. She told everyone at Red Rocks that even if it was their first time doing yoga, they belonged and shouldn't feel self-conscious or out of place. The mantra for the rest of the class was "I belong" and she encouraged all of us to use that mantra whenever we were trying something new or felt out of place. "I belong." Is a wonderful mantra to create an anchor to your super conscious mind. Mantras are an easy and effective way to battle negative self-talk and make positive connections. Different mantras will make sense to you on different days so feel free to mix and match mantras.

INTENTION

I am an intention enthusiast and believe that our intentions set our lives in motion either positively or negatively if we realize it or not. If we are living intentionally, we are aware that we are the creators of our life experience and not a victim to random outcomes. If our intentions are clear with ourselves, we are able to be clear with our intentions for others in our lives. Setting an intention is like setting a small goal each day. If the day doesn't go as intended, it is always good to reflect back to understand why. We unfortunately can't set intentions for others, but we can control how we react when our expectations and intentions are not met. Intentions should be focused on self-opposed to focused on controlling an outcome or person's actions. For example, a good daily intention would be "I intend to see the bright side in all situations at work today." An intention that wouldn't be as constructive would be "I intend to stay away from my psycho boss today." While you might not want to see your boss, chances are you will and if you are able to frame your intention in a positive open way, the chance for positive results will follow. Be intentional with your actions and your words and you will see a shift in your relationships very quickly.

MINDFULNESS

Mindfulness practices are ancient cross cultures all over the world in all religions and are now becoming main stream and are sweeping across our American culture with vitality and purpose. Corporations such as Google have created mindfulness spaces for their employees along with mindfulness classes and coaching to help employees create time to practice and manage stress during the workday. When I was working in the Public Sector, we brought in a wonderful mindfulness coach, Jule Lane, to help the department manage their high stress levels. Her insightful ideas on breathing and naming emotions helped provide tools for the teams to work through their high emotional stressers.

Even if you aren't lucky enough to work for one of these progressive establishments, you can do this easily on your own and this book will teach you how. I will give you ideas on how to make easy simple adjustments to your day that might seem trivial, but those adjustments, practiced over and over will create a new foundation for your life and stress management. We won't be able to eliminate stress from our lives, but the trick is to manage the good stress (preparing to graduate, have a baby, get a new job) and eliminate the stress that becomes negative like anxiety, hopelessness, and despair.

Studies show that mindfulness and meditation practices build and rebuild strong neuropathways in the brain for long lasting results to fight long term damage. Mindfulness is nothing new in the scheme of humanity and every religion from early Christianity to Buddhism uses mindfulness as a tool to connect, to heal, and to communicate. By definition, mindfulness is a mental state achieved by focusing one's awareness on the present moment, while calmly acknowledging and accepting one's feelings, thoughts, and bodily sensations. Many people I have worked with have shuttered at the word "mindfulness" because for them, the term is loaded with religious undertones. The fact of the matter, is mindfulness is just plugging your heart, mind, and body together to run as efficiently as possible. Whatever your spiritual preference is or lack thereof, the human being is complex and doesn't come with an owner's manual; we have to determine how to take care of ourselves with all the tools available – mindfulness practices are simply tools to keep the engine running smoothly and gas in the tank.

When you are living in the present moment, it is impossible to be filled with anxiety or depression. Anxiety is brought about when the mind is focused on the future which we all know has not happened yet so is it not real. When we are depressed, we are focused on the past of what has happened or what should have happened but didn't and again, is not real. This moment, the one right now, is real and has the ability to bring you joy and feelings of peace and calm if you choose to perceive it. Each of these moments then create your reality if you are conscious of it or not. Mindfulness brings your subconscious thought patterns to your conscious mind for you to either reinforce or change – it is the beauty of your free will.

Once you begin to live mindfully, you will reflect back on your former self and wish you would have made the switch sooner for everyone's sake.

TREAT YO'SELF – AKA- EAT THE TACOS

How often do we pass on the things that bring us the most joy? We limit our choices with thinking that is flawed like we don't deserve something nice, there are too many calories in tacos, we shouldn't indulge in buying things we love. We deny ourselves the tacos and then over indulge later. My advice after experiencing this pattern for years is have the tacos when you want the tacos and have a salad when you want a salad- stop denying what it is that brings you happiness. That goes for using the good linens, dishes, clothes, etc.. Why are you saving things for a special occasion? Make today your special occasion. Have tea using your special china you used with your grandma when she was alive, drink wine out of the crystal that your uncle brought back from Spain, set the table for dinner instead of eating over the sink (you know who you are). Ask yourself what you are saving and then ask yourself "why?" Why have nice things if they can't be enjoyed?

If there is something you would like to purchase, start saving for it if you can't afford it currently. Make a goal, put money towards it and see how good it feels to save for it. Take an empty spaghetti sauce jar, put a label on it, and start throwing all of your spare change into it to help save for it. When you see the jar filing up, it will bring you joy and excitement for the anticipation of achieving what you want to purchase and before you know it, voila – You will have it and will have that sense of joy opposed to feeling like you can never manifest the things you want. Dream big, and start small. Eat the tacos.

What a treat is to one person is not always a treat to someone else. What I have included in this book are either no cost or low cost ideas from my perspective which is limited by my own life experience and things I enjoy (please realize I don't get out much). Feel free to change any of the "Treat Yo'self" ideas to fit you. I highly encourage it actually because this is all for you. My suggestions may create a new idea for you or not. Don't le that stop you from treating yourself each day. It is an important practice to create and an important pattern to change if you are in the denial loop we all get in. My advice is to make each treat reasonable and simple and something you like not something someone else likes for you.

The treats you choose each day can be varying in size from lighting candles, taking a walk, to purchasing the thing you have been saving for – each day will bring new opportunities for treats. Use the concepts in this book to build your practice and before you know it, you will be an expert in knowing how to enjoy your life to its fullest.

HAIKUS

Oh how I love haikus. The haiku is a form of Japanese poetry that was invented by Matsuo Basho in the mid 17th century. Haikus are 3 lines with the first line being 5 syllables, the second line being 7 syllables, and the last line is 5 syllables again. Those are the only rules. I for some reason, have a strange ability to write and create haiku poems easily and over my life have found great joy in writing them and challenging others to write them with me. Haikus bring a smile to my face, and a sense of joy to my heart so I wanted to include haikus in the book. Conversely, my boys have over and over again declared how much they distain haiku poems. We all have different ways of creating joy (even if they are wrong - wink and smile). I hope my haikus make you smile and inspire you to find what creativity is within you be it poetry, painting, cooking, etc.. In all honesty, I wrote the haikus for the book before any other content because it brings me such joy (editing on the other hand, not joyful for me).

PHONE JOURNAL

We have our phones with us constantly for many reasons besides checking our Instagram account. We are attached to our phones now more than any other time in history. Some of us remember when our phones were actually connected to a wall. I know I could never have imagined what our phones have grown into with a new set of blessings and curses. We will attempt to use the phone for good with this activity and start a journaling practice each day.

Because you always have your phone, I thought it would be the best place to start your journaling activities. Use your phone to quickly and easily create, capture, and complain if needed. Create a note in your Notes app and title it "Joy Profile" or anything that makes sense to you. I designed a quick journaling activity each day that should take you maybe 2 - 5 minutes to complete. If you journal longer, awesome. Journaling is another way to be mindful and to process irrational thoughts easily without unloading then on the people in your life.

One idea to successfully incorporate a journaling practice, is as you open Facebook or Insta account on your phone, pause, do your journal work, and then go back to your social media. Easy! I want you do to this on your phone for a reason so if you keep a separate journal, I want you to try this for the time being. Note: If you are more comfortable writing in a notebook or paper journal, go.for. it. Feel free to write in this book as there is space left for you to jot down ideas in the "Phone Journal" sections. I want you to have instant access to write down your thoughts as they come to you and chances are high you will be close to your phone. Like the chances are really, really high. The intention of journaling is to give you an outlet to process thoughts, emotions, creativity, or anything that comes to mind. Journaling helps the mind process and find peace.

CREATING YOUR JOY PROFILE

We all have unique tastes, experiences, and gifts that need to be explored and celebrated. As we have touched on, what brings me joy might not be what brings you joy and we should all have the permission and expectation to create our own profile for joy. Joy shouldn't be an after-thought in our lives or a "nice to have." Joy is a "need to have" for survival on this planet and to use as a life preserver when we are in the throws of uncomfortable change, grief, and sadness. We focus so much on our physical selves and need to recognize we are more than that; we are complex highly intelligent beings with emotions, complex thought patterns, and connections to the Universe and all it encompasses. Joy is that connection to all aspects of ourselves exploding with good energy that expands beyond self to the world. Joyful expressions are contagious, like sneezes but much more powerful and welcomed.

If you feel like you aren't wired to be joyful, I will tell you that is false and is some belief you have created or perpetuated in your life. How your joy shows up is most likely different from others and that is completely reasonable. You may have negative associations with the word joy itself, and that is easy to fix as you work through your 28 days of activities. Make joy an experiment if you are science minded and see how your stress level changes with your practice.

An important component of creating your joy profile is to give. Give, give, give…compliments, smiles, kindness, and your time. All of these cost nothing and create amazing energy to demonstrate your divine nature.

The word "human" doesn't mean broken or less than. Humans are complex multidimensional evolving beings that have a need to be seen, heard, and understood. Think about that as you begin your joy practice. Where are or aren't you being seen, heard or understood? How is that impacting your joy? Your joy is your choice and your joy profile is your life's work and blueprint to creating your life preservers. It is great when people we love throw us a preserver, but it is even better when we can create our own.

THE POWER OF YOUR SMILE

Smile. Right now smile. You feel it throughout your face muscles, eyes, head, neck, and maybe even in your heart. Now, think of something funny that makes you chuckle or giggle. That simple act releases hormones in your body creating a great feeling and when you smile at or laugh with another person or group of people, you are connecting and bringing joy to yourself and everyone around you. How often do you smile? Do people give you compliments on your smile or how your smile makes them feel? Do an experiment this month and make a goal to smile more. Smile at people on the street, in traffic, at work, at school, at home – flash those pearly whites and see how that adds joy to your interactions and connections with others. Who knows, you just might smile at your soulmate and create new friendships.

Now, think of something that really makes you angry, then smile. You can't stay in that anger when you are physically smiling. Remember that as a "get out of anger free" card when you want to change an angry weather pattern.

BREATHING

Did you thank your breath for keeping you alive today? I know I never did before I started doing this work. My breath and water were far from my conscious thought but both have kept me alive since day one and continue to do so and deserve some serious gratitude. Our breath gives our mind signals to how our body is reacting to stress both good and bad, and our breath has the ability to calm our body down in extreme circumstances. Notice when you are upset or waiting for news if you hold your breath instead of breathing regularly. We gasp when we are shocked, and our breath is calm and centered when we are rocking a baby or playing with a puppy. Our breath is telling us about our well-being as well as creating our well-being at the same time. Take 3 really deep breaths as you read this and notice how your entire body feels the breath. Critical oxygen is flowing through your body and stagnant air is being released from your lungs. If you are outside and can take 3 deep breaths of fresh clean air, it connects you to nature and improves your heart rate. Breathing in essential oils using a diffuser or stopping to smell the roses really are great ways to be mindful of your breath and to create moments of joy. If you become stormy in your day, try taking 3-5 deep cleansing breaths and focus on the mantra for the day to become rebalanced. Give gratitude for clean air, your lungs, and your breath whenever you think of it.

SMALL ACTIONS – BIG RESULTS

I can't stress enough how important it is to put your thoughts in motion. You can sit and dream and connect to the Greater Good (which are all important), but without taking action to bring those dreams to this consciousness, you aren't fulfilling your purpose. You are meant to bring love and joy to this planet but if you constantly have a frown on your face, rush through your life holding your breath, and are completely stressed to a 10, you will never live your life's purpose not matter what your occupation.

If you choose instead to smile, breathe, let go, laugh, treat yourself well, that love and joy you are demonstrating will inspire others to do the same but most importantly, you will be showing yourself love and please believe me when I say you absolutely deserve it. Make a conscious decision to put your divine self in motion.

AS YOU BEGIN

Before you get started, I want to declare (and warn you) that this book is a reflection of me, my voice, my imperfections my dangling participles, split infinitives, crazy commas, and capitalizations, oh

CHAPTER 2
· EVERYDAY JOY AND ·
TACOS WEEK 1

This week begins your new journey to creating joy in your day. We will be focusing the work this week with the chakras from the root chakra to the crown chakra. Imagine that you are working from the bottom up, from your lower belly (root chakra) to the top of your head (crown chakra). The small activities focused on the chakras each day are meant to teach you about your energy so you can focus and get connected to each energy center one at a time a day at a time. Be aware of what messages come up each day, how you are feeling, and focus on creating moments of joy not only for yourself, but for everyone you encounter. Just a simple smile can do wonders for someone who is heartbroken. Enjoy you week, dig into the "Treat Yo'self" activities and make them your own because this is all about you and your personal definition of what brings you joy each day.

CHAKRAS

- **Monday - Root Chakra** – Lower abdomen - Red – Connection to earth – Sense of Survival

- **Tuesday** - **Sacral Chakra** – Mid abdomen - Orange - Creativity
- **Wednesday** - **Solar Plexus Chakra** – Mid body/ lungs - Yellow – Self Esteem and Self Confidence
- **Thursday** - **Heart Chakra** – Heart - Green, Pink, White - Love of self, love of others, love of all
- **Friday** - **Throat Chakra** – Neck - sky blue – Speak your truth
- **Saturday** - **3rd Eye Chakra**, Indigo – Middle of the forehead - Spiritual sight – Focus on intuition
- **Sunday** - **Crown Chakra** – Top of head - White – Connection to Spirit

NO. 1 – MONDAY – ROOT CHAKRA

FORECAST

100% certain to kick ass - Check in with your emotions in the AM and sweep away any irrational thoughts like the wind blowing clouds away. You are a powerful human being and deserve joy today.

MANTRA

I am brave. – This mantra is great when you realize it Monday and are feeling the Monday Monster or Monday Blues. When you are not feeling ready to transition out of weekend bliss into the Monday routine, remind yourself that you are brave and can take on not only a Monday, but can take on anything that comes your way today. You are brave and are creating a new practice by facing self-limiting patterns to replace them with joy and that is brave work my friend.

INTENTION

Today, my intention is to rise above the bullsh@t.

Anytime you feel sucked into drama or ego thinking, rise above it. Visualize floating above the situation and seeing it from a new perspective. Connect to and remain connected to your super conscious mind that is connected to your higher self and stay out of the bullsh@t. It isn't yours anyway so let go.

MINDFULNESS

Think about your breakfast, lunch, dinner, snacks. Consider where they came from, how many people had a part in bringing it to you including farming, transportation, grocery, etc. and be grateful for all of the energy that went into bringing you your food. Give this type of gratitude whenever you eat today.

TREAT YO'SELF

Get your best friend and go to your favorite coffee or tea shop. Catch up and laugh (a lot). If your best friend doesn't live near by, grab coffee and ask them to do the same. Facetime or call them and catch up. Don't let distance stop you in the super connected world we live in.

HAIKU

Replace taco with

Anything that makes you feel

Like you just won big

PHONE JOURNAL

What are your biggest triggers? Why do you think they are there?

NO. 2 – TUESDAY – SACRAL CHAKRA

FORECAST

100% certain to kick ass - Check in with your emotions in the AM and sweep away any irrational thoughts like the wind blowing clouds away. You are a powerful human being and deserve joy today.

MANTRA

I create – Human beings are creative and you are constantly creating your life experience. Many times we limit our concepts of creativity to art or music, but there are infinite ways to create your life. Use the mantra "I create" when you are writing an email, when you are thinking of a solution to a problem, or when you are smiling at someone. You are creating an experience and have the opportunity to create joy.

INTENTION

Today, my intention is to be grateful for all of the experiences that didn't end up going my way.

How many times have we bargained with the Greater Good about getting our way? "If you just give me this job, relationship, house, amount of money etc. I will be more (insert adjective). And how many times did we get angry when we didn't get what we were bargaining for? This cycle of "prayer" is flawed as we all have experienced and I suggest a new way to look at this cycle. Instead of asking for a bargain, instead declare your intention and then give gratitude for the best outcome for the highest good of everyone involved. The next step is to get out of the way and really release it to the Greater Good. That doesn't mean stop taking action, it means that you detach from an expected outcome, and open to the greatest possibility. I have had experiences in my life that when I got out of my own way and asked for the highest good for everyone involved, the outcome was better than anything I could have dreamed of. Along those same lines, think about the situations where you didn't get what you were hoping for, and now with a new perspective are so filled with gratitude that you didn't actually receive it. The Universe has an intelligence and unconditional love for us that we do not fully understand. If we can acknowledge that it does exist and believe in it, it will never disappoint.

MINDFULNESS

Make a conscious effort to not get upset in traffic. Let people in, wave and smile and notice the results in how your body feels when you arrive. Remember that we all make mistakes driving (some more than others) but let traffic slights go for your own peace of mind. I am guessing you may have made a mistake or 2 driving yo'self at some point (insert wink and smile).

TREAT YO'SELF

Taco Tuesday... 'Ole! Create a community Mexican Fiesta event with friends, family, neighbors and encourage everyone to contribute whatever they have on hand. Keep it simple and you will surprise yourself with what unique creations you can create. Creating community with food is one of deepest connections we can create and honestly, tacos aren't too shabby.

HAIKU

Powerful free will

If tacos give you heartburn

Find joy in sushi

PHONE JOURNAL

List 3 things to be grateful for today and feel deep gratitude in your being.

NO. 3 – WEDNESDAY – SOLAR PLEXUS CHAKRA

FORECAST

100% certain to kick ass - Check in with your emotions in the AM and sweep away any irrational thoughts like the wind blowing clouds away. You are a powerful human being and deserve joy today.

MANTRA

I will - The mantra "I will" is very powerful. You have free will and the power to make new choices in your life. When you say "I will" what follows needs to be in alignment with your true self and what you truly want or you will feel out of alignment. I will... meditate, I will...love, I will...create joy, smile, breathe, be kind, smell the roses, laugh opposed to I will never... love, win, succeed etc.. "I will" as a mantra is powerful.

INTENTION

Today, my intention is to let go of relationships that no longer serve me.

Please give yourself permission to look at the relationships in your life that bring you joy and those that take joy away. You have the ability to create your life and those people in it. Mentally detach from the drama generators in your life and see how you are able to breathe easier.

The hard part of this intention presents itself when family members are the drama generators in your life. Know that you can examine your relationship and how much energy you put into the relationship and how much joy and happiness you receive from the connection. If you need to take a break from listening to the same drama over and over, be kind to yourself and the person and take the break. Let them know that you are in the process of working on creating more joy in your life and need their help. You can kindly point out the constant drama and that you are wanting your conversations to focus on the positive things in your life opposed to everything that seems to be going wrong. They might not realize they are being negative or they might find someone else to complain to. Either way, win win!

MINDFULNESS

Imagine your emotions like the weather today. Let people know if it is going to be "stormy" and remember it is better to work through the emotion or storm, opposed to stuffing or ignoring it. Being prepared for a storm is much easier than being caught in it with no umbrella. Remember, everything is temporary and will pass. The sun does come out, that rain only makes us wet, and we do grow even when we are in the dark.

TREAT YO'SELF

Seek out cool artwork either locally or Google artists you love. Take time to look, appreciate, and buy a piece if it works with your budget. If you are inspired, treat yo'self to sometime creating your own masterpiece.

HAIKU

If tacos had wings
They would be a Pegasus
Magical belly

PHONE JOURNAL

Make 2 lists today of the people who inspire and are always there for you in your life, and a list of people who make you feel less than and are never there for you when times are tough. Start taking actions to have 0 people on that second list. You deserve to have a life filled with people who are rooting you on, just as you are there rooting on the people in your life.

NO. 4 - THURSDAY – HEART CHAKRA

FORECAST

100% certain to kick ass - Check in with your emotions in the AM and sweep away any irrational thoughts like the wind blowing clouds away. You are a powerful human being and deserve joy today.

MANTRA

I love - I love the "I love" mantra for so many reasons. Saying "I love" over and over is a great way to attract love to your life and create the connection to self-love. Where the "I love" mantra can be challenging is when you are at odds with someone and you have to use the "I love" mantra. It can protect you from yourself and can remind you that you actually do love the person who is driving you crazy. You might not love their actions, but at a level of human being, you love them. No one said joy was easy, right?

INTENTION

Today, my intention is to forgive anyone who triggers me, including myself.

Elusive, slippery forgiveness. We give forgiveness easily to some and refuse to give it to others. The action of forgiveness and letting go of past hurts is part of our human experience. It is a tool we have to process emotional and mental injuries and forgiveness has the capacity to heal ourselves and the others involved. Why then do we struggle forgiving? I believe the ego is the road block to forgiveness and we look many times at the ego as false protection. We believe that if we are unforgiving, we are setting boundaries and protecting ourselves from more hurt. The opposite is true. You can forgive a hurt and still have loving boundaries and can trust that you are protected by something bigger and greater than yourself. Forgiving yourself for bad decisions, reactions, or choices is imperative for you to heal. We all make the best decision we can at the time, and once we can accept things as they are and move on, we are able to forgive, detach and heal. Focus on forgiving everything you possibly can today and see what joy springs up.

MINDFULNESS

Take 3 deep breaths and meditate on the word "love." Think of all the love you have felt over your lifetime and who you give your love to. Imagine that expanding into past, present, and future connections and imagine it increasing exponentially. Make sure to give some of that love to yo'self.

TREAT YO'SELF

Chocolate in any color or quantity (unless you are allergic and if so, my heart goes out to you).

HAIKU

Happy heart is joy

Now you design what that means

Love, laughter, and light

PHONE JOURNAL

What does a perfect day look like to you? Who is with you and what are you doing? Get really specific so the Universe can respond with more of what you love.

NO. 5 – FRIDAY – THROAT CHAKRA

FORECAST

100% certain to kick ass - Check in with your emotions in the AM and sweep away any irrational thoughts like the wind blowing clouds away. You are a powerful human being and deserve joy today.

MANTRA

I speak - The Mantra "I speak" is helpful when there is something that needs to be said that you are putting off. When you start your day with the "I speak" mantra, examine where you are and aren't speaking up for yourself and understand why. You have every right to speak your truth and take a step towards your confidence by practicing this mantra today.

INTENTION

Today my intention is to listen more than I speak.

Make a point to speak less today and really tune into what people around you are saying and taking about. Listen actively to people you work and live with and notice what is being said in non-verbals like body language and heavy sighs. When you are actively listening, the people in your life want to share more and connect more with you. You may realize that you haven't really been listening to the people you love in your life.

MINDFULNESS

Watch your words today. If you become caught in a toxic conversation, acknowledge it and change the dynamic back to being positive. You will inspire others to do the same. If that isn't possible, smile and excuse yourself from the situation. You do not have to engage in negative behavior.

TREAT YO'SELF

Happy Friday! Make your favorite dinner for yourself and a friend or family member. use the "good stuff" you have been saving for a special occasion.

HAIKU

Do one thing that brings

Something new into your life

Small actions - big joy

PHONE JOURNAL

What holds you back from speaking your truth?

NO. 6 – SATURDAY – 3RD EYE CHAKRA

FORECAST

100% certain to kick ass - Check in with your emotions in the AM and sweep away any irrational thoughts like the wind blowing clouds away. You are a powerful human being and deserve joy today.

MANTRA

I see – The mantra "I see" is speaking to your intuition vs. your physical vision. Some examples are, "I see the good in you," "I see the love in that situation," "I see myself differently." Begin to develop and connect or reconnect to your intuitive self. Do not discount your intuition in situations and trust yourself. You have subtle warning signs all the time that are from your higher self either encouraging you or discouraging you protecting you from harm or bad decisions.

INTENTION

Today, my intention is to see my life through loving eyes.

Give yourself a big break today and when your inner critic flares up, remind yourself of your intention to see your life with love vs. unrealistic perfectionistic ego filters. You are unconditional love in motion.

MINDFULNESS

Meditate on your world perception. Envision a world where peace exists and there is no lack. Imagine you are in charge and can change anything you want and have the power to change it instantly. What would it impact? How would others react?

TREAT YO'SELF

How about some live music? A concert, street performers; you name it. If you can't get out, go on YouTube and discover some new talent for free or dig into the archives and listen to some of your old stuff. Music makes the heart happy.

HAIKU

Wherever you go

You are connected to all

Know that you belong

PHONE JOURNAL

What do you see yourself doing in 1 year, 3 years, 5 years?

NO. 7 - SUNDAY – CROWN CHAKRA

FORECAST

100% certain to kick ass - Check in with your emotions in the AM and sweep away any irrational thoughts like the wind blowing clouds away. You are a powerful human being and deserve joy today.

MANTRA

I am - Like the "I will" mantra, the "I am" mantra is very powerful. Anything that comes after the "I am" statement tells your conscious and logical brain something. If you are focusing on the mantra and you say "I am... powerful, I am... brave, I am... divine" these all are in alignment with your true self. If your mantra becomes "I am... not worthy, I am... stupid, I am...misunderstood, I am... broken, I am... never going to change" you can see how limiting the thinking and language becomes. "I am" is powerful.

INTENTION

Today, my intention is to stay connected to my guides and higher self.

How you might ask? Choose to pause and ask for guidance in situations that are unclear. Take deep breaths and remind yourself that you are indeed connected to something bigger than yourself and that something bigger loves you unconditionally.

MINDFULNESS

Meditate on the light of each human being. Imagine sharing your light like passing a flame from candle to candle to those that have let their fire go out. Do this while you are going about your day as well as in meditation. As you pass people, imagine passing a lit candle to them and smile.

TREAT YO'SELF

SLEEP IN as LATE as you want. It is Sunday Funday and let your body get the rest it needs. Have breakfast in bed, watch movies, read books, binge watch Netflix. Give yourself permission to have a low-key day and enjoy every minute.

HAIKU

We need each other

Asking for help is loving

Be open to joy

PHONE JOURNAL

Do you believe you are divine? If the answer is no, why? Side Note: The answer to this one is yes (wink and smile).

CHAPTER 3
· EVERYDAY JOY AND · TACOS WEEK 2

This week we are going to up it a notch and I believe you can absolutely handle it. There is a color associated with each chakra. This week, I would like you to focus on the color of the chakra of the day by counting it when you see it. For example, Monday your focus is your root chakra and the color associated is red. As you wake up, look at the red objects in your room, bathroom, kitchen, in traffic, at work, people's clothes etc.. You will see your day much differently when you are focusing on the color. This mindfulness exercise begins to train your brain to quickly focus. Ultimately, that focus you develop will be used to quickly see the good in situations that seem hopeless, see the silver linings easily, and focus on your true self consistently. You can use this mindfulness activity to calm down if you are triggered during your day. Happy week 2!

CHAKRAS

- **Monday - Root Chakra** – Lower abdomen - **Red** – Connection to earth – Sense of Survival

- **Tuesday** - **Sacral Chakra** – Mid abdomen - **Orange** - Creativity
- **Wednesday** - **Solar Plexus** – Mid body/ lungs - **Yellow** – Self Esteem and Self Confidence
- **Thursday** - **Heart Chakra** – Heart - **Green, Pink, White** - Love of self, love of others, love of all
- **Friday** - **Throat Chakra** – Neck - **Sky blue** – Speak your truth
- **Saturday** - **3rd Eye Chakra** – Middle Forehead - **Indigo** –- Spiritual sight – Focus on intuition
- **Sunday** - **Crown Chakra** – Top of head - **White** – Connection to Spirit

NO. 8 – MONDAY – ROOT CHAKRA

Forecast – 100% certain to kick ass - Check in with your emotions in the AM and sweep away any irrational thoughts like the wind blowing clouds away. You are a powerful human being and deserve joy today.

INTENTION

Today, my intention is to set healthy boundaries.

Setting boundaries are so important in all relationships and being able to determine, communicate, and keep those boundaries are each of our responsibility. You can detach from people that drain your energy and still love them and you can let go of the people in your life that are down right toxic. Set your intention today to create healthy boundaries and watch what happens.

MANTRA

I live – Pause for a moment and think about this. You are a living breathing, loving, human being on this planted and you LIVE. The mantra today is to remind you of how important your life is not only to yourself, but to those around you. You live and everyone in your life thanks you for it.

MINDFULNESS

Examine your belief around survival. What do you believe you need to survive? Are you a person who believes in abundance (that there will always be more) or are you a person who believes in scarcity (there will never be enough). We as humans are wired for the later and our reptilian brain is always on the lookout for threats to our survival (fight or flight). As we evolve, we are able to recognize those thoughts as irrational thinking and we are able to look around at our homes, jobs, communities, families, clean water, grocery stores and realize we are thriving not just surviving. Our root chakra is where we hold our energy that relates to survival. When we feel threatened, we feel a pit in our stomach or have other tummy related issues. We feel that worry in our guts. When we are able to shift from the scarcity thinking to abundant thinking and sweep away irrational thought, our entire being feels better and aligned.

TREAT YO'SELF

Hug more people, dogs, and or cats (if they will let you) today and see how it makes you feel. Hugging strangers might be too much to ask, but hug the people in your life a lot.

HAIKU

My dear you are love

Take it easy on yo'self

Eat tacos today

PHONE JOURNAL

What are your beliefs about success? Do you see yourself sabotaging your success or being afraid of both success and failure?

NO. 9 – TUESDAY – SACRAL CHAKRA

FORECAST

100% certain to kick ass - Check in with your emotions in the AM and sweep away any irrational thoughts like the wind blowing clouds away. You are a powerful human being and deserve joy today.

MANTRA

I heal – I am yet to meet someone that isn't healing, including children. Children are more open and honest about what they are healing and often times show you their scrapes, scars, and scabs with pride. We are healing in 4 dimensions all the time (physical, emotional, mental, spiritual) yet our physical healing gets the most attention. Imagine being hit by a truck and what would go into that scenario. An ambulance would take you away to a hospital, doctors and nurses would take care of you, your family would visit and take you home and care for you there. You would welcome the attention to healing knowing you can't do it on your own. Imagine that you have had an impact to your mental or emotional body as significant as being hit by a truck; maybe a divorce, a job loss, harassment, abuse, grief. How do you heal that injury? We are often lost and are told by others to "get over it" or are told "it isn't that bad" and are encouraged to bury it or not discuss it instead of heal it. Think about the scenario of physically being hit by the truck and instead of going in the ambulance, you limp away and people tell you to just "move on." You might have a limp and be handicaped your entire life because you don't stop to get help and heal. This is how we handle healing emotional, mental, and spiritual traumas right now and we can do better. We can acknowledge our pain, and be with others as they are healing their injuries. We are all healing from something and have the capacity to help the people we love heal by doing simple things like showing up and listening when needed. Your presence is more powerful than you can imagine.

INTENTION

Today, my intention is to do something kind for another person.

One of the things I love to do is to anonymously pay for lunch for someone who is eating alone or a young couple with a new family. A few extra dollars creates an experience where people remember just how good the world can be and makes the recipients feel loved and lucky. It is worth every penny trust me.

MINDFULNESS

When you feel triggered by a person or event, say to yourself "this is temporary" as many times as you need to feel centered again. All situations are temporary both good and bad so soak in the easy good feelings and events, and breath deep through the storms as they will always pass. It is always temporary.

TREAT YO'SELF

Walk in the grass, sand, snow, water with your bare feet. Feel nature and let that feeling heal any physical pain you might be experiencing – like frost bite if you are out in the snow.

HAIKU

You are beautiful
There is only one of you
See the light that shines

PHONE JOURNAL

Who do you need to forgive? Do you have a hard time letting go of other's mistakes? What make your mistakes less important that theirs?

NO. 10 – WEDNESDAY - SOLAR PLEXUS CHAKRA

FORECAST

100% certain to kick ass - Check in with your emotions in the AM and sweep away any irrational thoughts like the wind blowing clouds away. You are a powerful human being and deserve joy today.

MANTRA

I belong – Yes you sure do. You belong here. You belong exactly where you are and are important to a bigger design. You belong even when it isn't comfortable and you belong when it is comfortable. The mantra "I belong" helps you become more comfortable in your own skin. Say it over and over if and when you are feeling out of place today.

INTENTION

Today, my intention is to be kind to myself and not listen to my ego-inner critic.

No one has time for that noise; there is joy to be found and that inner-critic has no idea what that is. Your inner critic has had enough time in your ear and you can silence your inner critic by stepping into yourself and being happy. Happiness and joy silence that noise.

MINDFULNESS

Think of a problem you are working through in your life. Take a piece of paper and divide the paper in 2 parts. On one side write the word "Facts." On the other side write the word "Emotions." List all of the facts of the problem column and then jot down the emotions that are triggered. Separating the 2 will help you get clear on how to solve your problem and process your emotions. When we try to do it all at once, the facts get lost and the emotions can lead to irrational thinking. Find your inner Spock from Star Trek and see the problem from a logical point of view first. Once you do that, you might see things more clearly. It could be the emotional reaction you are feeling has nothing to do with the actual problem, but is a pattern that began at a different point in your life and you have a learned response. Acknowledge and heal the pattern by letting it go and choosing a different reaction and solution to your current problem.

TREAT YO'SELF

Get moving. Ride a bike, take a walk, start yoga (there are great classes on YouTube). Do any of these activities with a friend for bonus points.

HAIKU

Tacos filled with love

Shared in a community

Brings heaven to earth

PHONE JOURNAL

Do you believe that you create your life or that your life creates your circumstances? Do you believe if you were born into harsh circumstances that you can overcome them? Do you know of anyone who has overcome amazing odds to beat a disease, poverty, abuse, or neglect? Take inspiration from others and know you create your life every day.

NO. 11 - THURSDAY – HEART CHAKRA

FORECAST

100% certain to kick ass - Check in with your emotions in the AM and sweep away any irrational thoughts like the wind blowing clouds away. You are a powerful human being and deserve joy today.

MANTRA

Roll with It – Today's mantra is a "let it go" kind of mantra. Whatever happens in your day, roll with it. Do not let your joy or peace of mind be disturbed by other people's drama or storms. Roll with the circumstances of your day and hold onto your happiness by choosing it.

INTENTION

Today, my intention is to send love to myself, my tribe, state, country, and planet.

When you consciously send love out, your energy expands and it has a positive impact on everything around you. Imagine how powerful it would be for everyone on the planet to share this intention.

MINDFULNESS

Pick one person to send love to today. Think of them throughout the day having great success in their day and imagine them letting your amazing love energy into their being. Expert level challenge – send love to someone you are in conflict with or haven't been able to forgive.

TREAT YO'SELF

Splurge a little and make that purchase you keep putting off because you don't feel like you deserve it. You do deserve it (if you can afford it is a different question – wink and smile).

HAIKU

You made joy tacos
Worry is not invited
Love is your bouncer

PHONE JOURNAL

What do you love most about your life?

NO. 12 – FRIDAY –THROAT CHAKRA

FORECAST

100% certain to kick ass - Check in with your emotions in the AM and sweep away any irrational thoughts like the wind blowing clouds away. You are a powerful human being and deserve joy today.

MANTRA

I hear. – Today's mantra is very important for healthy relationships. So many times we listen to respond; we don't actually listen just to hear the other person. Focus on truly listening today. The person that drives you crazy at work, school, or home, take a deep breath and listen to their words, their body language, and hear them without feeling like you have to solve anything or respond. We all need to be heard (even the ones that seem off their rocker).

INTENTION

Today, my intention is to make sure my message is clear.

Do not assume everyone in your life understands what spins up in your mind. When you feel the phrase, "they should know!" coming out of your mouth, know that is a signal for you to pause and determine if you have actually told anyone what you think they should know. Make your message clear and ask the person to repeat back what you said so you are sure you were heard (in a kind way).

MINDFULNESS

Be aware of your word choices today. Whenever you begin to say "no" or negative phrases, be aware of why. Many times that is needed

("No, don't eat that Tide Pod) and other times we are saying "no" to opportunities because they are new and feel scary. Say "yes" whenever you can today even if it is a little scary and see where it leads.

TREAT YO'SELF

Buy yourself your favorite flowers (yes, even if you are a dude). Flowers have healing properties and bring beauty and joy for days. Buy a flowering plant if you are opposed to cut flowers. Literally stop and smell the roses today.

HAIKU

You are a rock star

Use your voice to sing your song

Music heals the world

PHONE JOURNAL

Who do you like to talk to the most and why? When was the last time you talked to them?

NO. 13 – SATURDAY – 3RD EYE CHAKRA

FORECAST

100% certain to kick ass - Check in with your emotions in the AM and sweep away any irrational thoughts like the wind blowing clouds away. You are a powerful human being and deserve joy today.

MANTRA

I perceive. – This mantra is key to understanding that we all have different points of view in our human experience. My perception is unique to my life experience as is yours. Both points of view are valid and our truth. If we are able to perceive the best in others, our outcomes will be more joyful for everyone.

INTENTION

Today, my intention is to see other perspectives in situations that I do not agree with.

This intention is a big one. Seeing the other perspective when the other perspective feels so wrong is a very hard thing to achieve. These days with our political climate completely polarized, the polarity adds a layer of frustration and a defeated feeling that is less than joyful. I know for myself, it is hard to hear the other perspective and to understand how anyone could see a different way on certain key issues like the climate, education, healthcare etc.. When I start feeling polarized, I think about very important people in my life and those people are my parents. My parents could be the only Republican, vegetarian, Metaphysical Christian, NRA members on this planet earth and I love them dearly. We definitely do not see eye to eye on most political issues, but I have learned to listen and understand where they are coming from and they (especially my dad) have given me the permission to make up my own mind without judgement and guilt; he actually encouraged me to become my own person. That gift is one I have worked to pass onto my own children and other people in my life I love dearly who have different beliefs. We can still love each other without creating more polarity thinking.

MINDFULNESS

Sit quietly, close your eyes, take 3 deep cleansing breaths and meditate on your perception of your past and present self. How have you changed and grown? What do you perceive your future self will be like?

TREAT YO'SELF

Go see a movie (or binge watch some NetFlix) with someone you love.

HAIKU

Can you see yourself
With new eyes focused on love
Precious gift of you

PHONE JOURNAL

What do you like most about the people in your life?

NO. 14 - SUNDAY – CROWN CHAKRA

FORECAST

100% certain to kick ass - Check in with your emotions in the AM and sweep away any irrational thoughts like the wind blowing clouds away. You are a powerful human being and deserve joy today.

MANTRA

I seek to understand. - Use this mantra over and over again today especially when things feel unclear. Be open to the answers to understanding situations deeper.

INTENTION

Today, my intention is to be open to guidance from the Greater Good.

When we plug ourselves into the energy that is bigger than ourselves, great things happen. We breath easier, we see things more clearly, and we are able to feel a sense of connection and calm. Think about a time when you felt the most connected to that energy and remember what was happening in your life. Be open to that guidance and support today; it will most likely come in unexpected ways.

MINDFULNESS

Open your mind as much as you can today to new ideas, new people, new information. The world is filled with beauty and new things to experience and all you need to do is open to the possibilities. Use your technology for good and Google a new topic today, a new vacation spot, a new restaurant, a new author heck, even a new word would work.

TREAT YO'SELF

Find a new fun neighborhood business and support them even if it is something simple like sharing their location on your social media outlets. Share a good review of them if you are so inclined and help support your local economy.

HAIKU

It takes light to grow
That light radiates in you
Shine shine shine shine shine

PHONE JOURNAL

Does your ego filter your spirit?

CHAPTER 4
· EVERYDAY JOY AND ·
TACOS WEEK 3

Week 3 introduces a new overlay of mindfulness techniques. The ask this week is to focus on the physical feelings of your chakras. For example, if you feel tightness in your lower abdomen, recognize that your root chakra is blocked and imagine white light healing that tightness. Ask yourself why you are feeling uncomfortable and do a quick Fact vs. Emotion exercise to get clear on why you are feeling uncomfortable if you aren't able to get to the root of it. Remind yourself that you live in an abundant universe and scarcity thinking is irrational. Breath deeply and name the abundance in your life (ex: home, family, education, clean water, freedom).

Repeat this type of mindfulness exercise with all of the other chakras this week. On the flip side, if you are feeling exceptionally healthy and happy, give gratitude for the increase in energy. Giving gratitude for the good brings more good. Happy week 3!

CHAKRAS

- **Monday - Root Chakra – Lower abdomen** - Red – Connection to earth – Sense of Survival
- **Tuesday** - **Sacral Chakra** – **Mid abdomen** - Orange - Creativity
- **Wednesday - Solar Plexus – Mid body/ lungs** - Yellow – Self Esteem and Self Confidence
- **Thursday** - **Heart Chakra** – **Heart** - Green, Pink, White - Love of self, love of others, love of all
- **Friday** - **Throat Chakra** – **Neck** - Sky blue – Speak your truth
- **Saturday** - **3rd Eye Chakra** – **Middle Forehead** - Indigo – Spiritual sight – Focus on intuition
- **Sunday** - **Crown Chakra** – **Top of head** - White – Connection to Spirit

NO. 15 – MONDAY – ROOT CHAKRA

FORECAST

100% certain to kick ass - Check in with your emotions in the AM and sweep away any irrational thoughts like the wind blowing clouds away. You are a powerful human being and deserve joy today.

MANTRA

Not my circus, not my monkeys. – I personally love this mantra. This is a great way to detach and set healthy boundaries. Do not allow yourself to get sucked into the drama of others. You won't be able to solve the issues and problems others create but you can love them through their bad choices without enabling or taking them on. You have our own circus to tend to.

INTENTION

Today, my intention is to take one action towards something that is out of my comfort zone.

Today is the day that you are going to be brave and take an action towards your dream. Make a plan, talk to an expert, do some research, set your dream in motion today and know you can do anything you set your mind to a day at a time. If we take our big dreams and break them in day to day chunks, they aren't overwhelming and become achievable. Get a little uncomfortable today and find joy outside of your comfort zone.

MINDFULNESS

Meditate in the morning on the topic of detaching. What do you have attachments to that no longer serve you? Realize that we all have coping mechanisms we learn at different stages in our lives that serve us at a point in time. When we were in elementary school, we weren't expected to do Calculus, we were just learning our numbers. So it is with our personal growth, we do what we know at the time and we continue to learn and grow. Evaluate what might not serve you any longer now that you are in a new phase in your life and let go of things that no longer bring you joy. You can honor what was without feeling guilty of past choices. We all do the best we can at the time and can always detach and change at any time to choose a happier healthier way.

TREAT YO'SELF

Eat your favorite snack regardless of calories today and enjoy every minute.

HAIKU

Mindful taco bite

Gratitude for this life

Thankful every day

PHONE JOURNAL

What makes you feel joy instantly?

NO. 16 – TUESDAY – SOLAR PLEXUS CHAKRA

FORECAST

100% certain to kick ass - Check in with your emotions in the AM and sweep away any irrational thoughts like the wind blowing clouds away. You are a powerful human being and deserve joy today.

MANTRA

I am whole. – We feel pulled in so many different directions with family, friends, work or school and we give our energy sometimes to a point we feel depleted. Focus on the mantra of "I am whole" today and see how it makes you feel. Does it feel authentic or forced? If it doesn't feel authentic, what is it that you feel is missing from being whole? Identify the lack, and imagine filling the void with love and white light to help heal the feeling.

INTENTION

Today, my intention is to call or text someone I have been meaning to reconnect with.

If it isn't obvious so far, connection is the secret sauce of joy. Think about someone in your life you have lost touch with but would love to catch up with. Spoiler, they are feeling the same way about you. Give them a call or shoot them a text.

MINDFULNESS

Mindful transitions are your focus today. Take 3 deep breaths when you wake up, before you go into school or your job, when you are leaving a building, when you enter your home, and before you go to bed. Think about the anxious energy we bring into buildings when we are hurrying through our day or if we are going places we don't really want to be. Doing the cleansing breaths before entering into a new space will help you feel more centered and calm wherever you go today.

TREAT YO'SELF

Get a massage, Reiki, pedicure, manicure (or DIY any of these). If you do not know what Reiki is, Reiki is a Japanese healing modality that puts your body in its most relaxed state to heal. It balances the chakras and is like acupressure mixed with a massage (you keep all of your clothes on). I highly recommend Reiki for people of all ages and am a Reiki practitioner myself. Google "Reiki Practitioner or Reiki Master" to find one in your area.

HAIKU

You radiate joy
And manifest every day
Create your best life

PHONE JOURNAL

What beliefs to do you have around money and survival?

NO. 17 – WEDNESDAY – SACRAL CHAKRA

FORECAST

100% certain to kick ass - Check in with your emotions in the AM and sweep away any irrational thoughts like the wind blowing clouds away. You are a powerful human being and deserve joy today.

MANTRA

I am fully protected. – I know for myself, the control freak in me hasn't easily let this mantra in. I don't easily trust situations at first (fight or flight baby) and I feel that I have to not only protect myself but also protect my family. The concept that I am fully protected by something bigger than myself was hard for me to wrap my mind around. Yet, when I reflect back on my life, I can easily see that I have been fully protected from making some extremely bad choices that would have put my life on a less joyful path. At the time, I didn't feel like I was being protected, rather, I felt defeated but in retrospect I can see how I was being protected by a greater intelligence that what I had at the time. Now whenever I feel unsettled or uneasy, I use the mantra when I am making a big decision and I connect to that higher intelligence.

INTENTION

Today, my intention is to create something new.

Create a vision board, a meal, a song, a sandwich, a painting, a poem, a meme, a new post, a cup of tea, create something that challenges you and brings a smile to your face.

MINDFULNESS

Eat with purpose and intention today. Do not distract yourself when you are eating. Do not look at your phone or rush and think about what you are eating while you enjoy your meal.

TREAT YO'SELF

Get online and pick a vacation destination. Dream up your next adventure and do some research. If it is within your power, book a trip to a new destination.

HAIKU

You belong right here
Special part of the design
There are no mistakes

PHONE JOURNAL

When I say "higher self" what does that mean to you?

NO. 18 - THURSDAY – HEART CHAKRA

FORECAST

100% certain to kick ass - Check in with your emotions in the AM and sweep away any irrational thoughts like the wind blowing clouds away. You are a powerful human being and deserve joy today.

MANTRA

I love life and life loves me. – This mantra sums it all up nicely. It is the ultimate relationship and state of consciousness we want to embrace. Declaring we love life and that life loves us back, we set in motion feeling of joy feelings of acceptance and that we love our lives as imperfect and flawed as they might be at times, we love our life and that life loves us back.

INTENTION

Today my intention is to take action to make sure everyone in my life knows they are loved.

From your perspective, what would a nice surprise be for you from your spouse, friends, or family? Would unexpected flowers make you feel loved, or maybe it would be just someone doing the dishes without you mentioning it. What can you do for others in your life to make them feel loved. Words are always great, but actions are even better. Think about how you can demonstrate how you love the people in your life today.

MINDFULNESS

Make a list of 3 things you are grateful for today. Be as specific as possible as to what they are and why they are important to you.

TREAT YO'SELF

Bake muffins, cookies, bread for the smell of it OR go to a bakery and treat yo'self!

HAIKU

Joyful heart be free

Connect to your higher self

Laugh at the past and let go

PHONE JOURNAL

What does unconditional love mean to you?

NO. 19 – FRIDAY – THROAT CHAKRA

FORECAST

100% certain to kick ass - Check in with your emotions in the AM and sweep away any irrational thoughts like the wind blowing clouds away. You are a powerful human being and deserve joy today.

MANTRA

So what? (up to 5 times in any situation). – This mantra feels sassy when you start but is a great way to disconnect from situations that either are out of your control, or no longer serve you. For example, let's say that your child (if you have children) didn't do their homework and you find out right before you are heading to school. Instead of getting upset with your child, say to yourself "so what". The answer will be something like, "he/she will get a lower grade". Then you ask yourself "so what" again. The answer will be along the lines of "he/she will learn a lesson to do their work." At the end of the "so what" searching, you realize that your hope is that you want your children to learn to do their work without you yelling at them so saying "so what" gives them the accountability to learn their lesson without you having to become triggered and impact your day and relationship. We think we have to solve and control so many things that are really not ours to solve, learn, or control. Our kids teach us that every day. They have their own journey with their own lessons, connections, joy, and injuries to heal. We as parents want to protect them from the world, but sometimes they need protection from our own reactions. Take a deep breath today and say "so what" as much as you can.

INTENTION

Today, my intention is to communicate from a place of power, because I am not a victim.

You are most definitely not a victim in your life and have the power to make changes every day. Changing your mindset to co-creator with the Universe feels much better than feeling held back, beaten down, and minimized. Today, focus on the power you do have or want to create in your life.

MINDFULNESS

Listen to yourself today in all of your conversations and interactions. Watch for filler words that make your message less powerful. Words and utterances such as "um, just, and like" introduce unnecessary pauses and tentative language in your communication. Make note if you are speaking your truth and delivering positive, constructive feedback to the people in your life. Be very intentional with how you are communicating today.

TREAT YO'SELF

Get your favorite gear (get something new if your budget allows) and go for a long walk or bike ride alone. Connect to nature, the sounds, smells and breathe deeply.

HAIKU

Speak your truth today

You will inspire others

Imagine THAT joy

PHONE JOURNAL

Do you consider yourself a good listener? Do people seek you out to listen to them?

NO. 20 – SATURDAY – 3RD EYE CHAKRA

FORECAST

100% certain to kick ass - Check in with your emotions in the AM and sweep away any irrational thoughts like the wind blowing clouds away. You are a powerful human being and deserve joy today.

MANTRA

I am the light. – Imagine a light that lives within you. Sometimes that light is dim when we are sad, sometimes that light is volcanic when we are angry, and sometimes that light shines through our eyes, smile, and body that inspires others and speaks to their light. Staying "lit" is an important part of creating joy. Not enough light it is hard to find the joy life preserver, too much light and the life preserver is burnt to a crisp. You have unlimited access to this light and your choice is to let it shine with love.

INTENTION

Today, my intention is to see my true potential.

MINDFULNESS

Look at someone who you do not get along with like they are your child. Can you empathize with them more easily?

TREAT YO'SELF

Look up some new styles and get a new outfit a little out of your comfort zone.

HAIKU

Imagine happy
Feel that happy deep inside
Give that happy life

PHONE JOURNAL

Do you hold yourself back from being your full self?

NO. 21 - SUNDAY – CROWN CHAKRA

FORECAST

100% certain to kick ass - Check in with your emotions in the AM and sweep away any irrational thoughts like the wind blowing clouds away. You are a powerful human being and deserve joy today.

MANTRA

I am valued. – You are precious to so many people and are valued greatly. We do not go around as much as we should telling people how valued they are so we lose sight of what we mean to the people in our lives. You are valued and this mantra today will help you reaffirm that you know that you are valued in all areas of your life.

INTENTION

Today, my intention is to put my life in action and to work towards something that moves me towards my life goals.

Take a small step, make a call, research, network, tell someone your dream. Whatever it is, take an action today towards your dream.

MINDFULNESS

Identify worries and triggers that are holding you back. Imagine them floating down a river away from you. Imagine white light filling your chakras with love, peace, and joy instead.

TREAT YO'SELF

Go for a new hairdo. up it a notch, hot towel, new style, extra conditioner. Do something special for yourself you don't normally do and let your stylist know you are working on creating more joy in your life.

HAIKU

Smile at sad eyes

That gift heals and inspires

Feel joy in your toes

PHONE JOURNAL

What was the most spiritual encounter you have had this far in your life?

CHAPTER 5
· EVERYDAY JOY AND ·
TACOS WEEK 4

You are in your final week of creating joy in your everyday life. This week the challenge is something that will require more of your imagination. Your imagination is not childish or insignificant; your imagination is connected to your super conscious thinking and to the Greater Good. I want you to imagine this week, as you design your day, that you are an archeologist digging for treasure and you will leave no rock unturned to find it. The treasure you are looking for is joy and your excavation site is you this week. Look for hidden joys in your routines, in your work day, in class if you are a student, at home with your family and add those buried joys to your joy profile. Happy week 4!

CHAKRAS

- **Monday - Root Chakra** – Lower abdomen - Red – **Connection to earth – Sense of Survival**
- **Tuesday** - **Sacral Chakra** – Mid abdomen - Orange - **Creativity**

- **Wednesday - Solar Plexus** – Mid body/ lungs - Yellow – **Self Esteem and Self Confidence**
- **Thursday - Heart Chakra** – Heart - Green, Pink, White - **Love of self, love of others, love of all**
- **Friday - Throat Chakra** – Neck - Sky blue – **Speak your truth**
- **Saturday - 3rd Eye Chakra** – Middle Forehead - Indigo – Spiritual sight – **Focus on intuition**
- **Sunday - Crown Chakra** – Top of head - White – **Connection to Spirit**

NO. 22 – MONDAY – ROOT CHAKRA

FORECAST

100% certain to kick ass - Check in with your emotions in the AM and sweep away any irrational thoughts like the wind blowing clouds away. You are a powerful human being and deserve joy today.

MANTRA

Suffering is optional. – As you experience your day, remember that you are designing it and if you are currently suffering in a situation, you can choose to make a change. Let's say for example you have a co-worker or friend who continuously vents all of their negative thinking to you. You begin to dread seeing that person because your interactions leave you feeling drained. Today, as you are saying your mantra to yourself, let this person know that you appreciate all they are going through, but would also like to talk about the good things happening in their life and share your mantra with them. Suffering is optional and is a signal to create a change.

INTENTION

Today my intention is to open up to new people.

When was the last time you made a new friend or let someone into your life? New people bring new perspectives and new connections means your tribe expands and you likelihood of creating joy increases.

MINDFULNESS

Feel your feet on the earth today. Watch how you walk and be conscious of how you walk when you are angry, vs. happy and joyful.

Your energy impacts everything around you if you are conscious of it or not. Be mindful of how you carry yourself today.

TREAT YO'SELF

Watch the sunrise or sunset. Take a picture to reflect on all of the beauty and share it with others.

HAIKU

Joy explodes each time

You shine that beautiful light

And share it with me

PHONE JOURNAL

What did you want to be as a kid? Are you doing any aspect of that now? If no, why not?

NO. 23 – TUESDAY SACRAL CHAKRA

FORECAST

100% certain to kick ass - Check in with your emotions in the AM and sweep away any irrational thoughts like the wind blowing clouds away. You are a powerful human being and deserve joy today.

MANTRA

I am infinite. – Today's mantra is a focus on your potential. We are infinite beings with infinite potential living in an infinite Universe. Believe in infinite possibilities of how to create joy in your day.

INTENTION

Today, my intention is to be grateful for where I am at in my life.

We will always be evolving. You can look at our bodies from the time we get here to when we leave and can we can all agree that they grow and change. Our emotional, mental, and spiritual bodies also grow and evolve. If we are able to pause and be grateful for our current stage in life, we are able to consciously assess what is going well and what we want to choose to improve.

MINDFULNESS

When you wake up, do a scan of your body to see what feels good and what doesn't feel so good. Imagine white light around all areas especially those that don't feel good. Keep that white light on those areas as you feel pain during the day.

TREAT YO'SELF

Burn candles before you go to bed and take 10 deep cleansing breaths to get any stagnant air and energy out of your body before you go to sleep.

HAIKU

See the best in all

Your eyes accept or reject

Do unto others

PHONE JOURNAL

What do you perceive as your greatest success to date?

NO. 24 – WEDNESDAY - SOLAR PLEXUS CHAKRA

Forecast – 100% certain to kick ass - Check in with your emotions in the AM and sweep away any irrational thoughts like the wind blowing clouds away. You are a powerful human being and deserve joy today.

MANTRA

I am worthy. – This mantra can trigger lots of emotions so be ready. You are worthy of love, kindness, laughter, joy. You are absolutely worthy. If you have had experiences in your life that have made you feel less than worthy, I invite you to imagine those all on a boat that you send to sea, and then Valhalla (set that boat on fire) to let all of those useless beliefs go. They do not serve you or your path to joy. Choose to believe and know that you are worthy of wonderful things.

INTENTION

Today, my intention is to stay connected to my higher self.

Your higher self, super conscious thought, whatever you want to call it knows a thing or 2. If you stay focused on your super conscious thinking, you will feel more creative, more connected to peace, and ultimately have a deeper sense of well-being.

MINDFULNESS

Sit quietly, close your eyes, and meditate on the idea of your higher self. What does she/he look like? Ask your higher self what you need to know at this stage in your life to live a full, joyful, well balanced life.

TREAT YO'SELF

Take a bath or shower extravaganza…new soap, bubble bath, salts, the works. Water is such an important part of our equation and we hardly pause to think about how important it is. Clean, running, hot and cold water in our homes, schools, work places are just expected now and are in our sub-conscious thinking (at least in the majority of America). Enjoy those bubbles!

HAIKU

Practice saying yes

To all the people you love

Begin to love all

PHONE JOURNAL

What do you believe your purpose is in life? If your answer is "I don't know", what do you love to do? Start there.

NO. 25 - THURSDAY - HEART CHAKRA

Forecast – 100% certain to kick ass - Check in with your emotions in the AM and sweep away any irrational thoughts like the wind blowing clouds away. You are a powerful human being and deserve joy today.

MANTRA

I have empathy. – Empathy for others is an important emotional intelligence factor to practice. When you can put yourself in someone else's shoes and feel for their issues and problems, it makes you a more compassionate person and will help guide your actions. Without empathy, it is almost impossible to make connections with others.

INTENTION

Today, my intention is to smile more at others, including strangers and people I don't necessarily like.

As I have mentioned, smiling does wonders for your own health and well-being. It also impacts those around you and encourages them to smile as well. It is harder to smile at those that you have issues with, but if you can rise above the current conflict, imagine them as someone's child, and know that taking the higher road will always make you feel better in the long run even if the climb to that higher road is steep. Smile.

MINDFULNESS

Make a list of all that you have accomplished in your life thus far and give yourself some of that love you have been giving others and the world. Fill up your cup by remembering all you have accomplished this far. No one has had the same life experience or set of circumstances to overcome and learn from. Well done you!

TREAT YO'SELF

Wash your face AM and PM with an extra hot towel like they do at the spa. Add essential oil if you have any around for some easy aroma therapy.

HAIKU

Gratitude today
Say thank you for the small things
More good things will come

PHONE JOURNAL

What makes your heart happy?

NO. 26 – FRIDAY – THROAT CHAKRA

FORECAST

100% certain to kick ass - Check in with your emotions in the AM and sweep away any irrational thoughts like the wind blowing clouds away. You are a powerful human being and deserve joy today.

MANTRA

Yes I can do it. – Whatever "it" is for you, do it today. Put your thoughts and joy in motion. If you are hesitant to make a decision, say yes and DO IT. Do not wait, do not stop yourself, just take a step into what you know you need to do. Say "yes" to yourself today.

INTENTION

Today, my intention is to inspire others to speak their truth in a positive, effective, loving way.

Inspiring others is no easy task. Leading by example is a great way to inspire people. You can also encourage someone in your life that needs to speak up for themselves to do it and reassure them they have your support. As Mahatma Gandhi so wisely told us, "be the change you wish to see in the world." By just being your authentic self, you will inspire others to do the same.

MINDFULNESS

Connect with a friend or family member and let them know how much they mean to you. How many points in our days allow for deep connection with people we admire or have changed the course of our lives? We can create this easily by sending an unexpected text, email, phone call, sharing a photo on social media with a great memory. Connect today to the person who is your person. Making sure they are feeling appreciated is important.

TREAT YO'SELF

Listen to or watch something that makes you laugh…a lot. Look up babies laughing, cat videos (if that is your thing), and get in some belly laughs.

HAIKU

Focusing on self

Is not selfish or ego

It is your purpose

PHONE JOURNAL

Who makes you laugh the most?

NO. 27 – SATURDAY – 3RD EYE CHAKRA

FORECAST

100% certain to kick ass - Check in with your emotions in the AM and sweep away any irrational thoughts like the wind blowing clouds away. You are a powerful human being and deserve joy today.

MANTRA

As within, so without. – This mantra is a perception changer. The concept is that your internal feelings are also expressed in your external life. If you are feeling peaceful and centered internally, your life is in balance externally. If your internal life is struggling, so will your external. As you look at your day, say the mantra to yourself and see how it applies. When you are feeling centered driving in traffic, do you let people in and continue listening to your 80's hair band music (brings me joy and brings my family pain) or do you grip your steering wheel tighter, cut people off because they should have known you were merging, and swear. In those cases, I invite you to pause and think about where your head is at. Are you taking a bad day at work out on traffic, is it just a pattern you have created over time whenever you get in the driver's seat? As within, so without.

INTENTION

Today, my intention is to visualize the next version of myself and give gratitude for achieving it.

Connect to that important imagination today and think about what it will feel like when you have achieved the goals you are setting in your life. It could be anything from graduating, a new career, a partner, family, a creative project, not swearing at your children or friends, whatever your goal visualize that you have achieved it and feel gratitude in your being for the achievement.

MINDFULNESS

See your part in any conflicts you have during your day. Realize you are always creating your life and walk away from creating conflict whenever you can. I have found that it is much better for everyone if I can decompress my own way away from the conflict so I don't go volcanic on the other person or people. There is always more damage control to do after a conflict that goes poorly. That being said, constructive conversations over differences is much different than deliberately engaging in conflict. If you aren't sure what the difference is, do the "Truth vs. Emotion" exercise to get clear on the origin of what you are working on. Save yourself from conflict wherever you can today.

TREAT YO'SELF

Take a road trip (bike, car, bus, train) explore something new. If you can, create a ditch day and spend the day exploring.

HAIKU

Gorgeous human friend

Do not be afraid to grow

You are powerful

PHONE JOURNAL

Do you see yourself the same way other people see you? What are 3 words people would use to describe you?

NO. 28 - SUNDAY – CROWN CHAKRA

FORECAST

100% certain to kick ass - Check in with your emotions in the AM and sweep away any irrational thoughts like the wind blowing clouds away. You are a powerful human being and deserve joy today.

MANTRA

I am divine. – Channel your inner Beyonce' and know that you are a divine being. We all come from a divine presence a divine love so powerful we are yet to fully understand just how divine love is and how divine we are. Use this mantra over and over even if you don't fully believe it yet. Plant the seeds of your divine nature and watch them grow.

INTENTION

Today, my intention is to choose joy and create joy in all interactions.

Choose it today. Make this day your grand finale of joy. Feel it in your heart, wear a smile on your face, radiate your amazing energy and inspire people to say to themselves, "I want that to be like that!"

MINDFULNESS

Write a letter to yourself today to explain this month and your journey to finding deeper joy. Write about your "Ah ha!" moments, what was hard to process, and what was easy for you. Look back on your phone journals for the past 28 days and include anything in your letter to yourself that has to do with goals, your plans for the next year, 3 years, or 5 years. Make a commitment to yourself to read that letter a year from when you write it to see what has happened. Set an appointment on your calendar on your phone so you don't forget.

TREAT YO'SELF

Do some yoga, go dancing, shake your grove thing in your PJs if that brings you joy. Your body will thank you.

HAIKU

Set clear boundaries
Banish negativity
Kindness starts with you

PHONE JOURNAL

How can you tell when you are balanced and centered?

CHAPTER 6
· CONCLUSION – ·
WRAPPING IT ALL UP

YOUR NEW PRACTICE

My hope for you is that the past 28 days were fun, challenging, and broke the concept of joy open to see a different facet and perspective. My wish for you is that you continue down this path of mindful living to create your best self and the best life you continue to dream up. I hope you have new confidence, new dreams, and a new or renewed sense of connection to the people in your life, to the greater good, and to yourself. Take these activities and modify them for your next months and build onto them and share them with others in your life. You did a lot of great work in a short amount of time and I hope you feel a sense of pride in your accomplishment.

YOUR OWN RESEARCH

We live in a world now where you can get answers to your questions instantly. Google has made life's big mysteries easier to solve with a simple search bar. If anything I have included in this book has made you want to dig deeper, please Google it, seek out answers to your questions, find teachers and continue down the path of self-discovery and self-love.

I have been blessed with countless teachers, but the one that truly helped me realize my passion for mindfulness and meditation was my Meditation teacher Janet Williams. She is the most modest person and will roll her eyes when she reads this, but I cannot imagine what my life would be like if I would not have opened up to take her Meditation 101 class so many years ago now. Open your experience to new teachers, research what you find interesting, and take action to put yourself out there for all of us to experience. You are protected, you are divine, and you will bring joy to the world by just being in it.

ALL ABOUT YOU

At the end of the day, your life is all about you. It really is. If you choose to put yourself in the center of your universe and realize that your thoughts create your actions which create your life, you realize you do have the ability to create a life all about you in a loving way. If your life is all about you and you are all about joy, you create a world that we all want to be a part of and connected to. Choosing yourself and choosing joy becomes a habit, a pattern, and then inspires others to do the same. If we all live with joy, imagine the shift in our world. It is completely possible; you just did it for the past 28 days. Well done you!

SO MUCH MORE

As I write my final thoughts, I am sitting next to my newly decorated Christmas tree, enjoying a roaring fire in my fireplace, Christmas jams quietly playing in the background with my two dogs guarding my feet. I am finishing "Everyday Joy and Tacos" during the

Christmas season this year which couldn't be more perfect and it makes me reflect on my elementary school middle name taunters. There is a good chance my childhood perception was flawed and they were actually foreshadowing my future life's passion of bringing joy to this world. I believe that each of us is unique, precious, important and powerful deserving a life that is filled with unconditional love. I hope I meet you one day and you share with me your journey to discovering your joy. There is so much more to experience, so much more to say, and so much more to do but for now, I hope you choose to smile, to breathe deeply, and eat the tacos; you deserve joy every day.

ACTIVITY TABLES

The tables included below are for you to mark-up, circle, cross out, star, whatever works for you to identify what you like and to identify anything that doesn't resonate. They can also be an easy reference as you are building your practice to see all of the mantras, intentions, mindfulness activities, and phone journal ideas at a glance. The majority of these are included in the book, and there are a few new ones in the tables below. As always, make them your own to get the maximum benefit.

MANTRAS

Chakra	Day of Week	Week 1	Week 2	Week 3	Week 4
Root	Monday	I am brave.	I thrive.	I choose abundance.	I am protected.
Sacral	Tuesday	I create.	I heal.	I am whole.	I am infinite.
Solar Plexus	Wednesday	I will.	I belong.	Roll with it.	I am worthy.
Heart	Thursday	I love.	Not my circus, not my monkeys.	I love life and it loves me.	I have empathy.
Throat	Friday	I speak.	I hear.	So what?	My voice matters.
3rd Eye	Sat	I see.	I perceive.	I choose to see clearly.	As within, so without.
Crown	Sun	I am.	I understand.	I chose to connect.	I am divine.

MINDFULNESS ACTIVITIES

Chakra	Day of Week	Week 1	Week 2	Week 3	Week 4
Root	Monday	Think about your breakfast. Consider where it came from, how many people had a part in bringing it to you including farming, transportation, grocery, etc. and be grateful for all of the energy that went into bringing you your breakfast. Give this type of gratitude whenever you think about it today.	Look for the color red today throughout the day. Doing mindfulness exercises like this help build focus.	Meditate in the morning on the topic of abundance. Connect with your higher self and understand what fears need to be removed if any around abundance vs. scarcity.	Feel your feet on the earth today. Watch how you walk and be conscious of how you walk when you are angry, vs. happy and joyful.

MINDFULNESS ACTIVITIES

Chakra	Day of Week	Week 1	Week 2	Week 3	Week 4
Sacral	Tuesday	Make a conscious effort to not get upset in traffic. Let people in, wave and smile and notice the results.	When you feel triggered by a person or event, say "this is temporary" to yourself as many times as you need to feel centered again.	Take 10 deep breaths when you wake up, before you go into school or your job, when you are leaving, and before you go to bed.	When you wake up, do a scan of your body to see what feels good and what doesn't feel so good. Imagine white light around all areas especially those that don't feel good. Keep that white light on those areas as you feel pain during the day.

MINDFULNESS ACTIVITIES

Chakra	Day of Week	Week 1	Week 2	Week 3	Week 4
Solar Plexus	Wednesday	Imagine your emotions like the weather today. Let people know if it is going to be "stormy" and remember it is better to work through the emotion or storm, opposed to stuffing it. Being prepared for a storm is much easier than being caught in it with no umbrella. Remember, everything is temporary and will pass. The sun does come out.	Think of a problem you are working through in your life. Take a piece of paper and divide the paper in 2 parts. On once side write the word "Facts". On the other side write the word "Emotions". List all of the facts in the problem and then the emotions. Separating the 2 will help you get clear on how to solve your problem and process your emotions.	Do not distract yourself when you are eating today. Do not look at your phone or rush while you are eating.	Drink 120 oz of water today. Say the word "health" over and over to yourself or out loud if you can when you drink the water.

MINDFULNESS ACTIVITIES

Chakra	Day of Week	Week 1	Week 2	Week 3	Week 4
Heart	Thursday	Meditate on the word "love". Think of all the love you have felt over your lifetime and who you give your love to. Imagine that increasing exponentially and feel how great that feels.	Pick one person to send love to today. Think of them throughout the day having great success in their day and letting that great love energy in.	Make a list of 3 things you are grateful for today. Be as specific as possible as to what they are and why they are important to you.	Make a list of all that you have accomplished in your life and give yourself some of that amazing love you have been giving others and the world. Fill up your cup.
Throat	Friday	Watch your words today. If you become caught in a toxic conversation, acknowledge it and change the dynamic back to being positive. You will inspire others to do the same. If that isn't possible, excuse yourself.	Communicate your boundaries today. If you need to say "no" do so with kindness and know that you cannot make everyone happy and you are the only one who owns your own happiness.	Listen to yourself today. Be very intentional with how you are communicating.	Connect with a friend or family member and let them know how much they mean to you.

MINDFULNESS ACTIVITIES

Chakra	Day of Week	Week 1	Week 2	Week 3	Week 4
3rd Eye	Sat	Meditate on your world perception. Envision a world where peace exists and there is no lack.	Do something kind for someone else anonymously. Pay for the coffee for the next person in line, leave a treat for your co-worker, pick up trash etc.	Look at someone who you do not get along with like they are your child. Can you empathize with them more easily?	See your part in any conflicts you have during your day. Realize you are always creating your life and walk away from creating conflict whenever you can.
Crown	Sun	Meditate on the light of each human being. Imagine sharing your light like passing a flame from candle to candle to those that have let their fire go out.	Open your mind as much as you can today to new ideas, new people, new information. The world is filled with beauty and new things to experience and all you need to do is open to the possibilities.	Identify worries and triggers that are holding you back. Imagine them floating down a river away from you. Imagine white light filling your chakras with love and peace and joy instead.	Give thanks to the Greater Good in everything you do today. For waking, showering, driving, working, playing, laughing, eating etc. Say "Thank you" 100 times before you go to bed.

TREAT YO'SELF IDEAS

Chakra	Day of Week	Week 1	Week 2	Week 3	Week 4
Root	Monday	Stop and really smell the roses, aroma therapy, breathe it in.	Hug more people, dogs, cats etc.	Eat your favorite snack regardless of calories	Watch the sunrise or sunset. Take a picture to reflect on how beautiful it was.
Sacral	Tuesday	Um…Taco Tuesday 'ole! Create a community event with whatever is in everyone's kitchen.	Walk in the grass, sand, snow, water with your bare feet if possible.	Get a massage, Reiki, pedicure, manicure (or DIY any of these)	Burn candles before you go to bed.
Solar Plexus	Wednesday	Seek out cool artwork (and buy a piece if it works with your budget)	Call a friend and go get coffee or a bite.	Get in nature…own yard, park, travel and see it through new eyes.	Take a bath or shower extravaganza…new soap, bubble bath, salts, the works.

TREAT YO'SELF IDEAS

Chakra	Day of Week	Week 1	Week 2	Week 3	Week 4
Heart	Thursday	CHOCOLATE (unless you are allergic and if so, my heart goes out to you).	Splurge a little and make that purchase you keep putting off. You actually do deserve it.	Bake muffins, cookies, bread for the smell of it OR go to a bakery and treat yo'self!	Wash your face AM and PM with a hot towel like they do at the spa. Add essential oil if you have any around.
Throat	Friday	Make your favorite dinner for yourself and a friend. use the "good stuff" you have been saving for a special occasion.	Buy yourself your favorite flowers…Yes even if you are a dude.	Go for a long walk or bike ride alone.	Listen to or watch something that makes you laugh…a lot.
3rd Eye	Sat	Live music…Concert, street performers, etc.	Go see a movie (or binge watch) with someone you love.	Look up some new styles and get a new outfit a little out of your comfort zone.	Take a road trip (bike, car, bus, train) explore something new.
Crown	Sun	SLEEP IN as LATE as you want.	Find a new fun neighborhood business.	Haircut… up it a notch, hot towel, new style, extra conditioner etc.	Do some yoga, go dancing, shake your grove thing. Your body will thank you.

JOURNAL TOPICS

Chakra	Day of Week	Week 1	Week 2	Week 3	Week 4
Root	Monday	Triggers	Belief on success	Belief on failure	What did you want to be as a kid?
Sacral	Tuesday	3 things to be grateful for	Who do you need to forgive?	Belief on abundance	What does success look like?
Solar Plexus	Wednesday	Who is your person and why?	Belief on manifesting and creating	Belief about your higher self	Belief about your purpose in life
Heart	Thursday	What is a perfect day?	What do you love most about your life?	What does unconditional love mean to you?	What makes your heart happy?
Throat	Friday	What holds you back from speaking your truth?	Who do you like to talk to the most?	Do you consider yourself a good listener?	What makes you laugh?
3rd Eye	Sat	What do you see yourself doing in 1 year, 3 years, 5 years.	What do you like most about the people in your life?	Do you hold yourself back from being your full self?	Do you see yourself the same way other people see you?

JOURNAL TOPICS

Chakra	Day of Week	Week 1	Week 2	Week 3	Week 4
Crown	Sun	Do you believe you are divine?	Does your ego filter your spirit?	What was the most spiritual encounter you have had this far in your life?	How can you tell you are balanced and centered?

SETTING INTENTIONS

Chakra	Day of Week	Week 1	Week 2	Week 3	Week 4
Root	Monday	Today, my intention is to rise above the bulls@&t.	Today, my intention is to set healthy boundaries.	Today, my intention is to take one action towards something that will give me a sense of security.	Today my intention is to open up to new people.
Sacral	Tuesday	Today, my intention is to be grateful for all of the experiences that didn't end up going my way.	Today, my intention is to do something kind for another person.	Today, my intention is to call someone I have been meaning to reconnect with.	Today, my intention is to be grateful for where I am at in my life.

SETTING INTENTIONS

Chakra	Day of Week	Week 1	Week 2	Week 3	Week 4
Solar Plexus	Wednesday	Today, my intention is to let go of relationships that no longer serve me.	Today, my intention is to be kind to myself and not listen to my ego-inner critic.	Today, my intention is to create something new.	Today, my intention is to stay connected to my higher self.
Heart	Thursday	Today, my intention is to forgive anyone who triggers me, including myself.	Today, my intention is to send love to my tribe, state, country, and planet.	Today my intention is to take action to make sure everyone in my life knows they are loved.	Today, my intention is to find something or someone new to love.
Throat	Friday	Today my intention is to listen more than I speak.	Today, my intention is to make sure my message is clear.	Today, my intention is to communicate from a place of power, not victim.	Today, my intention is to inspire others to speak their truth in a positive, effective, loving way.
3rd Eye	Sat	Today, my intention is to see my life through loving eyes.	Today, my intention is to see the other perspective.	Today, my intention is to see my true potential.	Today, my intention is to visualize the next version of myself and give gratitude for it being done.

SETTING INTENTIONS

Chakra	Day of Week	Week 1	Week 2	Week 3	Week 4
Crown	Sun	Today, my intention is to stay connected to my guides and higher self.	Today, my intention is to be open to guidance from the Greater Good.	Today, my intention is to put my life in action and so something that moves towards life goals.	Today, my intention is to choose and create joy in all interactions.

Printed in the United States
By Bookmasters